The Lighthouse Companion
for
Long Island Sound

Photographs by Paul Rezendes

Tide-mark Press
Windsor, Connecticut

Text design by Paul Rasid
Maps by Dan Veale/AMV Graphics

ISBN 1-59490-025-6
Library of Congress Control Number 2005926206

First Edition/First Printing
Printed in Korea

Execution Rocks Lighthouse

The legend of Execution Rocks is, as might be expected, a grisly one. It is said that during the Revolutionary War British soldiers tortured American patriots at this outpost approximately 1 mile north of Sands Point. The prisoners were then bound to the rocks and drowned when the tide came in. Because of the site's disturbing history, any keeper who requested a transfer out was immediately granted one without question.

This rocky ledge is the site of Execution Rocks Lighthouse, established in 1850. The 60-foot tower was designed by prominent architect Alexander Parris, though at that time it didn't have its distinctive brown-and-white color scheme; the brown band on the tower did not appear until 1895. In 1856 a fourth-order Fresnel lens replaced the previous 13 lamps with red reflectors. In 1867 a two-and-a-half-story granite keeper's dwelling was added.

In December 1918 a fire at Execution Rocks Lighthouse significantly damaged the station, destroying the oil house and engine room and singeing the exterior of the light tower. The cause of the blaze was never identified, but the light continued to operate without interruption.

Execution Rocks Lighthouse was automated in 1979 and continues to serve as an active aid to navigation with a modern solar-powered optic that exhib-

Sands Point, Long Island, N

Directions

Execution Rocks Lighthouse is located directly offshore from Sands Point. It can be viewed from a few lighthouse cruises, including the Long Island Lighthouse Society's annual Gold Coast Lighthouse Cruise held each May. Call the Society at (631) 207-4331 for more information.

Latitude: 40°52'42"N
Longitude: 73°44'18"W

Contact Information:
U.S. Coast Guard Group/
MSO Long Island Sound
Aids to Navigation Team
120 Woodward Avenue
New Haven, CT 06512
(203) 468-4510
www.uscg.mil/d1/units/grumsolis/

Contents

Eaton's Neck Light

Long Island Sound Lighthouses

In the 18th and 19th centuries, fishing and whaling were primary industries for the people of Long Island. The peninsula's lighthouses, therefore, were critical in sustaining the good fiscal health of its communities. In addition to assisting fishers and whalers throughout the centuries, Long Island's beacons have served as a warm welcome to visitors from both near and far—in fact, until the Statue of Liberty was erected in 1886, Montauk Lighthouse, New York's oldest lighthouse, was often a transatlantic visitor's first glimpse of America.

Though Montauk may be the best-known of the 17 existing Long Island lighthouses, each shares an equally important role in assisting mariners today, as they have done for centuries. And each has a compelling story behind it. One was built on the site of a former Revolutionary War killing ground, one is said to be haunted by the ghost of a former keeper, and one belongs to its own self-declared nation that comes complete with its own currency, navy, and "joint chiefs of ice cream" (Ben Cohen and Jerry Greenfield of Ben & Jerry's ice cream fame).

Through incredible efforts, Long Islanders have restored many of the towers from the brink of destruction. Yes, Long Islanders are passionate about their light stations—and we hope that after reading the story of each, you will be too.

Connecticut, meanwhile, has enjoyed a long maritime history due to its location on Long Island Sound and the presence of the Connecticut River. Native Americans, the state's first residents, used its waterways for transportation and sustenance. Commercial vessels used in the trading industry sailed here as early as the 17th century and were later replaced with a steamboat service that ran from New York City to Hartford. By the 18th and 19th centuries, shipbuilding had become one of the state's largest industries.

Lighthouses first began to appear on the Connecticut coast in 1823, when the Stonington Harbor Lighthouse was erected on Windmill Point. Since then, there have been 23 beacons built on the shoreline of the "Charter Oak State," 21 of which are still active. As you will see in the following pages, the stories of Connecticut's lighthouses are imbued with history, a sense of romance, and even the occasional ghost.

Long Island Sound Lighthouse Locations by Number

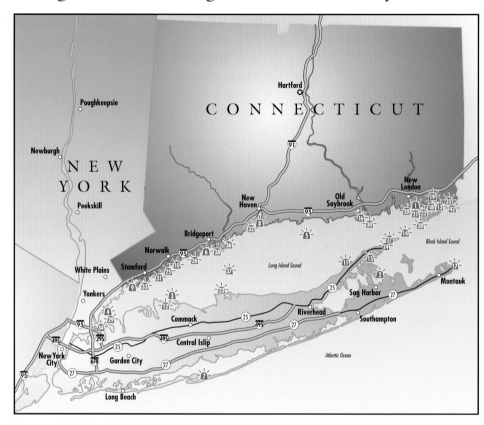

Avery Point Lighthouse

The last lighthouse built in Connecticut, Avery Point Lighthouse was constructed on United States Coast Guard grounds as a ceremonial light tower serving as a symbol of the Coast Guard's work with lighthouses and the sea. First lit on May 2, 1944, Avery Point Lighthouse initially exhibited a fixed white light, which was changed to a flashing green beacon on March 3, 1960.

Avery Point Lighthouse

Groton, Connecticut

The 55-foot tower was operated privately until the Coast Guard left the area on June 25, 1967, at which point the light was extinguished. In 1997, officials from the University of Connecticut at Avery Point campus, which now surrounds the lighthouse, called for a restoration of the deteriorating tower. The Avery Point Lighthouse Society, a chapter of the American Lighthouse Foundation, was formed in 2000 to raise funds for the effort. In December 2001, the tower's lantern room was removed, but renovation of the tower did not begin until September 2003, due to a lack of funding. Restoration efforts are currently in progress; the Avery Point Lighthouse Society hopes to relight the tower by October 2005 and eventually house a historical museum in the tower's first floor.

Directions

Take I-95 to exit 87 (CT 349, Clarence B. Sharp Highway) in Groton. Turn right at the second traffic light onto Rainville Avenue. Turn left at the next light onto Benham Road. Continue straight for approximately 1.7 miles to the University of Connecticut at Avery Point. Take the second entrance and drive straight toward the water. Parking is available in front of the Project Oceanology building.

Latitude: 41°18'55"N
Longitude: 72°03'49"W

Contact Information:
Avery Point Lighthouse Society
P.O. Box 1552
Groton, CT 06340
(860) 445-5417
www.averypointlight.com

Cedar Island Light

Though now a quaint and quiet town, Sag Harbor was once one of the Northeast's busiest whaling ports, attracting maritime traffic from all over the world. Often, the giant whaling ships traveling to and from the port experienced difficulty in maneuvering the narrow passage between Cedar Island and Shelter Island. To aid mariners, a light station was first established in 1839, 200 yards offshore on Cedar Island, so named because of the lovely cedar grove there. The first lighthouse was 35 feet tall, built of wood, and topped with a cast-iron lantern. In 1855, Cedar Island Light became the first light station on Long Island to receive a Fresnel lens when a sixth-order lens was installed to replace the original nine lamps with 14-inch reflectors.

Fewer than 30 years after the first lighthouse was established, a 40-foot, four-story granite light station and integrated two-and-a-half-story keeper's quarters replaced the wooden tower in 1868. The following years saw the addition of a fog signal (1882) and an oil house (1902) to the site.

In 1903 the Lighthouse Board turned its attention to the quickly eroding Cedar Island; roughly half of the three-acre island had disappeared since the light station was first established. To thwart the elements, riprap—a sustaining wall of stone thrown together without order—was placed on the north and west sides of the island. By 1907 more than 6,000 tons of riprap had been laid.

Cedar Island Light

Also known as Cedar Point Light
Sag Harbor, Long Island, New York

In 1934 Cedar Island Light was decommissioned and left to the harsh elements of nature. It was sold into private ownership in 1937 and one year later was landlubbed when the Hurricane of 1938 filled in the small strait of water separating Cedar Island from the coast and turned the island into a peninsula.

In 1967 Suffolk County purchased the light and turned the property into a county park. However, in 1974 a fire badly damaged Cedar Island Light's beacon and destroyed the station's roof and interior. After years of neglect and vandalism, on March 23, 2002, Suffolk County and the Long Island Chapter of the U.S. Lighthouse Society announced their partnership to restore and preserve Cedar Island Light. The group is actively working to return this historic landmark to its former glory.

Directions

Cedar Island Light is located in Cedar Point County Park in East Hampton. To get there, take Montauk Highway to Stephen Hands Path in East Hampton. Turn north and continue to Old North West Road. Bear left and continue to Alewive Brook Road. The park entrance is nearly 100 yards down the road.

Latitude: 41°02'27"N
Longitude: 72°15'41"W

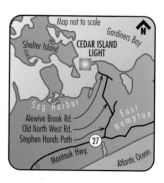

Contact Information:
Long Island Chapter,
U.S. Lighthouse Society
P.O. Box 744
Patchogue, NY 11772
(631) 207-4331
www.lilighthousesociety.org

Eaton's Neck Light

More than 200 shipwrecks have occurred on the submerged rock reef off Eaton's Neck Point. Though the owner of the point, John Gardiner, had erected an oil lamp on a pole to warn unsuspecting mariners, the government decided a more substantial warning system was in order and purchased 10 acres from Gardiner for $500 in 1798 to establish a light station. Upon its lighting on January 1, 1799, Eaton's Neck Light became the second-oldest lighthouse on Long Island.

Eaton's Neck Light

Huntington, Long Island, New York

Designed by John McComb Jr., the 73-foot-tall octagonal fieldstone structure still towers over Long Island Sound today from its perch on a hill. Eventually the beacon's single oil lamp was deemed inadequate, and in 1838 12 lamps with 13-inch reflectors were installed. Twenty years later, the lamps were replaced with a third-order Fresnel lens, which continues to shine today.

In 1868 the tower was lined with brick reinforcements and a fog signal was added on the grounds. Eaton's Neck Light was automated in 1968 and continues to serve as an active aid to navigation for the U.S. Coast Guard. The original keeper's quarters have since been replaced by Coast Guard housing.

Directions

From Highway 25A in Vernon Valley, take Waterside Avenue north for 1.5 miles and turn left onto Eaton's Neck Road. After about 1 mile, Eaton's Neck Road becomes Asharoken Avenue. Travel 3 miles, and turn right onto Lighthouse Road. The Coast Guard Station at Eaton's Neck is at the end of the road. The station is closed to the public; visitors are allowed by appointment only.

Latitude: 41°57'12"N
Longitude: 73°26'36"N

Contact Information:
U.S. Coast Guard Station
Eaton's Neck
12 Lighthouse Road
Northport, NY 11768
(631) 261-6959
www.attheneck.com

Execution Rocks Lighthouse

The legend of Execution Rocks is, as might be expected, a grisly one. It is said that during the Revolutionary War British soldiers tortured American patriots at this outpost approximately 1 mile north of Sands Point. The prisoners were then bound to the rocks and drowned when the tide came in. Because of the site's disturbing history, any keeper who requested a transfer out was immediately granted one without question.

This rocky ledge is the site of Execution Rocks Lighthouse, established in 1850. The 60-foot tower was designed by prominent architect Alexander Parris, though at that time it didn't have its distinctive brown-and-white color scheme; the brown band on the tower did not appear until 1895. In 1856 a fourth-order Fresnel lens replaced the previous 13 lamps with red reflectors. In 1867 a two-and-a-half-story granite keeper's dwelling was added.

In December 1918 a fire at Execution Rocks Lighthouse significantly damaged the station, destroying the oil house and engine room and singeing the exterior of the light tower. The cause of the blaze was never identified, but the light continued to operate without interruption.

Execution Rocks Lighthouse was automated in 1979 and continues to serve as an active aid to navigation with a modern solar-powered optic that exhibits a white flash every 10 seconds.

Execution Rocks Lighthouse

Sands Point, Long Island, New York

Directions

Execution Rocks Lighthouse is located directly offshore from Sands Point. It can be viewed from a few lighthouse cruises, including the Long Island Lighthouse Society's annual Gold Coast Lighthouse Cruise held each May. Call the Society at (631) 207-4331 for more information.

Latitude: 40°52'42"N
Longitude: 73°44'18"W

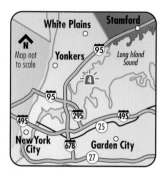

Contact Information:
U.S. Coast Guard Group/
MSO Long Island Sound
Aids to Navigation Team
120 Woodward Avenue
New Haven, CT 06512
(203) 468-4510
www.uscg.mil/d1/units/grumsolis/

Faulkners Island Light

Originally called Falcon Island by the British because of the many falcons that once resided here, Faulkners Island lies approximately 3 miles south of Guilford Harbor. In 1802 President Thomas Jefferson commissioned a lighthouse and wooden keeper's house to be built on the island, and Faulkners Island Light became the second lighthouse in Connecticut. Built by stonemason Abisha Woodward (who also built New London Harbor Light), the brick-lined tower stands 46 feet tall.

One of Faulkners Island's most famous keepers was Captain Oliver Brooks, who served from 1851 to 1882. Throughout his 31 years of service, Captain Brooks attended to approximately 100 ships. After rescuing five passengers from the wrecked schooner *Moses F. Webb* in November 1858, he was awarded a gold medal by the New York Life Saving Society.

The keeper's house was replaced in 1871 with an eight-room, three-story structure. Unfortunately, the house burned down in 1976 and the fire caused extensive damage to the tower as well; the lighthouse was decommissioned as a result. The light was repaired and automated in 1978.

Due to erosion, the light now stands approximately 35 feet from the edge of the island. Thanks to the nonprofit organization Faulkners Light Brigade, the lighthouse was completely restored in late 1999 and erosion control measures have been implemented by the Army Corps of Engineers. Faulkners Island Light continues to serve as an active aid to navigation, flashing a white beam every 10 seconds.

In September 2002, Faulkners Island Light celebrated its bicentennial with an open house and fireworks display that drew nearly 1,000 visitors, including Coast Guard staff and former keepers who served at the light.

Directions

Faulkners Island Light is accessible by boat only. The island has been designated as a bird sanctuary and is closed to the public during nesting season. Faulkners Light Brigade holds annual open houses of the lighthouse in September; call the organization at (203) 453-8400 for more information. The lighthouse can also be seen distantly from Guilford. *From I-95 North or South*: Take exit 58 and follow CT 77 (Church Street) into Guilford Center. Turn right on Broad Street, then left on Whitfield, and follow to a marina with free parking. The lighthouse can be seen to the south.

Latitude: 41°12'42"N
Longitude: 72°39'12"W

Contact Information:
Faulkners Light Brigade
P.O. Box 199
Guilford, Connecticut 06437
(203) 453-8400

Fayerweather Island Light

In 1807, the government purchased 9.5 acres of land from David Fayerweather for the purpose of building a lighthouse to mark the entrance of Black Rock Harbor. The 40-foot octagonal tower was completed the following year but was destroyed in a hurricane in 1821.

Architects of the second lighthouse, completed in 1822, were determined to build a tower that would withstand rough weather conditions. An 1850 inspection found that the tower was as effective as the builders intended. A new lantern was installed and a fifth-order Fresnel lens replaced the previous eight oil lamps.

One of Fayerweather Island Light's most notable keepers was Catherine Moore. Moore began assisting her father, keeper Stephen Moore, at age 12.

Fayerweather Island Light

Also known as Black Rock Harbor Light
Bridgeport, Connecticut

When she was 24, her father was injured and she served as unofficial keeper for the next 52 years. During her tenure as keeper, Catherine Moore saved 21 lives.

After its decommissioning in 1933, the lighthouse was given to the city of Bridgeport and became part of the town's Seaside Park. The lighthouse suffered decades of neglect and vandalism until two local residents established the Fayerweather Island Restoration Fund in 1993. Thanks to their efforts, the tower has been repainted and relit. According to the Fayerweather Island Restoration Fund that continues to work to improve the lighthouse, public tours and historical plaques may be in the tower's future.

Directions

From I-95 North or South: Take exit 26, and bear right onto Admiral Street. Turn right on Iranistan Avenue, and right again at Sound View Drive onto P. T. Barnum Boulevard, which you follow to the park. There is a charge to enter the park. Follow Barnum Boulevard to a parking area near a fishing pier and the sand spit leading onto Fayerweather Island. It's about a 20-minute walk to the lighthouse.

Latitude: 41°08'32"N
Longitude: 73°13'02"W

Contact Information:
Fayerweather Island
Restoration Fund
c/o Burroughs Community Center
2470 Fairfield Avenue
Bridgeport, CT 06605
(203) 334-0293

Fire Island Light

A whaling port, a bohemian retreat, a haven for the wealthy—Fire Island has had a long and varied history since its discovery in 1653. One important chapter in the island's life began in 1826, when a lighthouse was first established. At only 74 feet, the original octagonal tower was disregarded for being too short and was replaced in 1857 with a 168-foot red brick tower equipped with a first-order Fresnel lens.

The circular foundation of the original tower is still visible, and stone from that tower was used in the construction of the new beacon's terrace. It is said that the ghost of a keeper who hanged himself in the original tower still haunts the property, opening and closing heavy doors and windows and causing other eerie disruptions.

Fire Island Light

Fire Island National Seashore, Long Island, New York

Note: Though not on Long Island Sound, Fire Island Light is located on Long Island.

Fire Island Light was electrified in 1938 and automated and decommissioned in 1974. After learning of the Coast Guard's plans to demolish the landmark, a group of citizens formed the Fire Island Lighthouse Preservation Society in 1982. Since its inception, the group has had the lighthouse placed on the National Historic Register and restored the tower to its 1939 condition. Through the efforts of the group, Fire Island Lighthouse was relighted and reinstated as an active aid to navigation on May 28, 1986.

Today, though the Coast Guard maintains the light, the property is managed by the Fire Island Lighthouse Preservation Society. A museum is housed in the former keeper's quarters, and tours of the lighthouse are available.

Directions

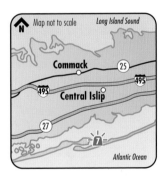

Fire Island Light is located on Long Island's southern shore, at the western end of the Fire Island National Seashore, just east of Robert Moses State Park. To get there, take the Long Island Expressway to exit 53, and follow the signs to Robert Moses State Park. Proceed to parking area #5. There may be a fee to park, depending on the time of year you visit.

Latitude: 40°37'54"N
Longitude: 73°13'06"W

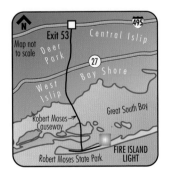

Contact Information:
Fire Island Lighthouse
Preservation Society
Box 4640
Captree Island, NY 11702
(631) 321-7028
www.fireislandlighthouse.com

Five Mile Point Lighthouse

One of New England's most prosperous cities, New Haven was a hub of coastal and West Indies trade in the early 19th century. The first lighthouse was built here in 1805 and was nicknamed Five Mile Point Light, to represent the distance it stood from downtown New Haven. From its inception, the 30-foot light was considered too short and too dim. To add to its problems, trees in the area began to obstruct views of the lighthouse's signal.

The current beacon was built in 1840 to replace the obsolete 1805 structure. It stands 70 feet tall and is built of sandstone from East Haven and lined with brick from New Haven. The attached keeper's dwelling is painted red. The lighthouse's 12 lamps and reflectors were replaced with a fourth-order Fresnel lens in 1855, and a fog bell was added a few years later.

Five Mile Point Lighthouse

Also known as New Haven Harbor Light
New Haven, Connecticut

When the Southwest Ledge Light was activated in 1877, Five Mile Point Lighthouse was discontinued. Today it is owned by the city of New Haven and stands in Lighthouse Point Park near the city's only public swimming beach.

Directions

From I-95 North or South, take exit 50N or 51S to Townsend Avenue. Follow signs for Lighthouse Point Park to Lighthouse Road, and turn right into the entrance to the park.

Latitude: 41°14'57"N
Longitude: 72°54'13"W

Contact Information:
Lighthouse Point Park
Lighthouse Road
New Haven, CT 06515
(203) 946-8005
http://cityofnewhaven.com/parks/
parks/lighthousepoint.htm

Great Captain Island Lighthouse

Great Captain Island lies approximately 1 mile off the coast of the town of Greenwich. Open only to Greenwich residents, the 17-acre property is home to a picnic area, beaches, and a lagoon. Local legend states that the island is also thought to be home to Captain Kidd's buried treasure.

The original lighthouse and five-room keeper's cottage were built in 1829 on the southeast end of the island. Inspections over the next few decades proved that the lighthouse was poorly constructed: walls were cracked and windows often leaked. Although a new fourth-order Fresnel lens installed in 1858 improved the dim lighting inside the lighthouse, the decision was made to replace the building.

Great Captain Island Lighthouse

Greenwich, Connecticut

A stone lighthouse was built on the same spot in 1868. It was fitted with the previous structure's fourth-order Fresnel and received a fog whistle in 1890. In 1907, a steam whistle replaced the original fog signal. Later a compressed air siren was installed. Great Captain Island Lighthouse was automated in 1970, but a caretaker still resides in the keeper's house to prevent vandalism.

In 1998 the Greenwich Chamber of Commerce started a campaign to relight Great Captain Island Light. Fundraising for the tower's restoration is ongoing.

Directions

The lighthouse cannot be seen from the mainland. There is a ferry to the island for Greenwich residents only; call (203) 622-7818 for information. The lighthouse may be visible from some lighthouse cruises (see Appendix).

Latitude: 40°58'54"N
Longitude: 73°37'24"W

Contact Information:
Greenwich Town Hall
101 Field Point Road
Greenwich, CT 06830
(203) 622-7814

Greens Ledge Light

This sparkplug-style light was commissioned by the government in 1896 to mark the entrance to Norwalk Harbor. Completed in 1902 at a cost of approximately $60,000, Greens Ledge Light was originally fitted with a fifth-order Fresnel lens that exhibited a flashing red light. The lantern soon was upgraded to a fourth-order lens that exhibited a white light interspersed with red flashes.

Greens Ledge Light was automated in 1972 and fitted with a modern rotating lens. The light and accompanying fog signal continue to serve as active navigation aids under the auspices of the U.S. Coast Guard.

Greens Ledge Light

Norwalk, Connecticut

Directions

From I-95 North, take exit 12 to CT 136. Follow CT 136 for about 0.5 mile, then turn right on Roton Avenue. Bear left onto connecting Pine Point Road, then turn right on Pine Point Terrace. Turn left at Gull Road, then right at Ensign Road. Turn left at Crescent Beach Road and continue onto South Beach Drive. The lighthouse can be seen offshore as you drive along the beach. It can also be seen distantly from the ferry from Norwalk to Sheffield Island. Call the Norwalk Seaport Association at (203) 838-9444 for more information.

Latitude: 41°02'30"N
Longitude: 73°26'36"W

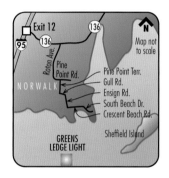

Contact Information:
U.S. Coast Guard Group/
MSO Long Island Sound
120 Woodward Avenue
New Haven, CT 06512
(800) 774-8724

Horton Point Lighthouse

Horton Point Lighthouse stands high on a cliff over the town of Southold and was named for Barnabus Horton, an Englishman who was one of the town's founding fathers and most prominent residents.

Though only 58 feet tall, Horton Point Lighthouse emits a flashing green light from a modern optic that shines at 103 feet above sea level. George Washington recommended a light station be built here in 1790, but it wasn't until the middle of the 19th century that the government acquired eight acres of land for the beacon. In 1857 the 58-foot granite tower and detached brick keeper's quarters were completed at a cost of $7,500, and William

Horton Point Lighthouse

Southold, Long Island, New York

Sinclair, who helped construct the buildings, was hired as the station's first keeper. A third-order Fresnel lens was installed, and on June 4, 1857, Horton Point Light became an active aid to navigation with a fixed white light.

In 1933, the station was deactivated and replaced by a skeleton tower. The tower was used by the military as an observation post during World War II but fell into disrepair during successive decades. In 1990 the Southold Parks District, which owns the property, partnered with the Southold Historical Society and the Coast Guard to restore the light tower. After extensive renovations, including repainting the interior and exterior of the tower, installing new glass in the lantern room and a new stairway, and making electrical repairs throughout the property, Horton Point Lighthouse was reinstated as an active aid to navigation on June 9, 1990.

Today, a nautical museum resides in the keeper's quarters, and tours of the tower are available.

Directions

From Highway 25 or Route 48 in Southold, turn north on Youngs Avenue. Turn right on Old North Road, and then make a quick left onto Lighthouse Road, which will lead directly to the lighthouse.

Latitude: 41°05'06"N
Longitude: 72°26'48"W

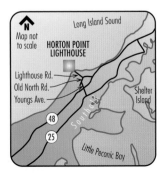

Contact Information:
Southold Historical Society
P.O. Box 1
Southold, NY 11971
(631) 765-5500
www.southoldhistoricalsociety.org

Huntington Harbor Light

Huntington Harbor Light is perhaps best known for its distinctive architecture—the 42-foot tower established in 1912 was designed in the Beaux Arts style, making it look more like an ancient castle than a 20th-century lighthouse.

This magnificent structure replaced a previous tower built in 1857 on a point at the end of East Beach known as Lloyd's Neck. Lloyd Harbor Light guided mariners into Lloyd Harbor but was ineffective to those entering and exiting nearby Huntington Harbor. Huntington Harbor Light, though located in the inner harbor rather than on Lloyd's Neck, services both harbors, but is often referred to as Lloyd Harbor Light as a result.

Huntington Harbor Light was considered a difficult station for keepers. The tower held two lighting devices—a fifth-order Fresnel lens and an Argand lamp—that needed to be maintained daily. In addition, the station had no electricity, running water, or indoor plumbing. Because of this, keepers' families were housed in the dwelling attached to the inoperational Lloyd Harbor Light.

Huntington Harbor Light

Also known as Lloyd Harbor Light
Huntington, Long Island, New York

In 1949, Huntington Harbor Light was automated. In the early 1980s, after more than 30 years of neglect, the lighthouse was deemed unsafe by the U.S. Coast Guard and scheduled to be demolished. A group of citizens stepped in and formed Save Huntington's Lighthouse, Inc. The group has since restored the tower and plans to open a museum in the building.

Directions

The lighthouse is accessible by boat only, but it is open for tours from May through October. Call the Huntington Lighthouse Preservation Society for schedules and directions to the dock.

Latitude: 40°54'36"N
Longitude: 73°25'54"W

Contact Information:
Huntington Lighthouse
Preservation Society
P.O. Box 2454
Halesite, NY 11743
(631) 421-1238
www.huntingtonlighthouse.org

Latimer Reef Light

Though often thought to be a Connecticut lighthouse because of its location just 4 miles south of Mystic, Latimer Reef Light is located in New York waters.

First established in 1844, Latimer Reef Light succeeds many other warning signals created to warn mariners of the dangerous reef off Fishers Island Sound. An iron spindle and buoy stood here as early as 1800, but a more notable signal was that of the Eel Grass Shoal Lightship, which served less than a mile northwest of the present lighthouse for approximately 35 years. Upon the establishment of Latimer Reef Light on July 1, 1884, the Eel Grass Shoal Lightship was deactivated; the ship's captain, Charles E. P. Noyes, was named keeper at the new sparkplug-style station.

Latimer Reef Light

Fishers Island Sound, Fishers Island, New York

Constructed of cast iron and lined with brick, Latimer Reef Light consists of three stories of keeper's quarters, a watch room, and a lantern room. The tower stands 49 feet tall and was originally fitted with a fifth-order Fresnel lens. In 1899 Latimer Reef Light was upgraded to a fourth-order Fresnel lens, and in 1974 the light became automated. Nine years later, in 1983, the tower's Fresnel lens was removed and replaced with a 300-mm modern optic that emits a flashing white signal every six seconds. Latimer Reef Light continues to be an active aid to navigation, making it the oldest cast-iron beacon still in use by the First Coast Guard District.

Directions

Latimer Reef Light is located on the northeast tip of Fishers Island and is best viewed by boat. See Appendix for charter information. The station is not open to the public.

Latitude: 41°18'18"N
Longitude: 71°56'00"W

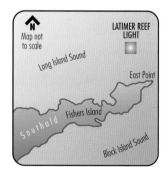

Contact Information:
U.S. Coast Guard Group/
MSO Long Island Sound
Aids to Navigation Team
120 Woodward Avenue
New Haven, CT 06512
(203) 468-4510
www.uscg.mil/d1/units/grumsolis/

Little Gull Island Light

Little Gull Island Light serves to warn mariners of the dangerous area where Long Island Sound and Block Island Sound meet. Known as "The Race," this treacherous area of water has claimed several vessels and the lives of many of those onboard.

Little Gull Island Light was first established in 1804. The original stone tower was 50 feet tall and constructed at a cost of $15,000. Conditions at the station were not amicable. Little Gull Island was an isolated location and visitors to the lighthouse were rare. In addition, the island was solid rock, with no fertile land for gardening or farming. Lastly, there was no well and no fresh water supplied to the island. Keepers were required to filter rain water or travel to Great Gull Island to obtain water from the well there.

On September 23, 1815, Little Gull Island was hit by a hurricane. The light-house keeper was on the mainland, but the keeper's wife and four children

Orient Point, Long Island, New York

weathered the storm, which badly damaged the station's buildings and swept away much of the island.

In 1869 the present 81-foot granite tower was constructed and a second-order Fresnel lens was installed. In 1978 the light was automated. In 1995 a modern 350-mm optic replaced the second-order lens, which has since been displayed at the East End Seaport Maritime Museum in Greenport, New York. Though the two-and-a-half-story keeper's house has been demolished, the tower still serves as an active aid to navigation, exhibiting a flashing white light every 15 seconds.

Directions

Little Gull Island Light is not open to the public, but it can be viewed from one of several charters or tours (see Appendix).

Latitude: 41°12'24"N
Longitude: 72°06'30"W

Contact Information:
U.S. Coast Guard Group/
MSO Long Island Sound
Aids to Navigation Team
120 Woodward Avenue
New Haven, CT 06512
(203) 468-4510
www.uscg.mil/d1/units/grumsolis/

Long Beach Bar Light

Long Beach Bar Light is located on a rock pile to the west of Long Beach Point to mark the entrance to Orient Harbor. Affectionately known as "Bug Light" because of its resemblance to a bug floating on the water, Long Beach Bar Light was first lit on December 1, 1871. The ornate Victorian structure was constructed on a screwpile foundation, and it was this metal framework that comprised the "legs" of the bug.

The screwpile foundation was replaced by a concrete foundation in 1926 that allowed for a new central heating system to be installed. Bug Light was decommissioned in 1943. Twenty years later, on July 4, vandals set fire to the structure and completely destroyed it.

Long Beach Bar Light existed only as ruins until 1990, when the East End Seaport and Marine Foundation raised more than $140,000 and hundreds of people came together to rebuild the landmark. Full reconstruction of the original wooden octagonal beacon rising from a square two-story keeper's

Long Beach Bar Light

Also known as Bug Light
Orient Harbor, Long Island, New York

house was completed in a mere 60 days, and the lighthouse was relighted on September 5 of that same year.

Today, the property is jointly managed by the East End Seaport Museum and the U.S. Coast Guard. It serves as an active aid to navigation with a 250-mm optic flashing a white light every four seconds at 63 feet above sea level.

Directions

Though best viewed from the water, Long Beach Bar Light can be seen from Orient Beach State Park. To get there, take the Long Island Express-way (Route 495) east to the end, then follow Route 25 east to the park.

Latitude: 41°06'34"N
Longitude: 72°18'21"W

Contact Information:
East End Seaport Museum
and Marine Foundation
P.O. Box 624
Greenport, NY 11944
(631) 477-2100
www.eastendseaport.org

Lynde Point Light

First lit on August 17, 1803, Lynde Point Light was built to mark the entrance to the Connecticut River. The wooden tower stood 35 feet tall and was octagonal in shape. By 1838, however, the original tower was replaced with the current 65-foot brownstone structure. Although similar masonry was used in the construction of nearby New London Harbor and Faulkners Island lighthouses, Lynde Point is thought to be the finest example of the three.

A seawall was constructed around the tower in 1829 to combat erosion from strong river currents and was widened and reinforced three years later. In 1852 the lighthouse's system of 10 lamps and reflectors was replaced by a fourth-order Fresnel lens. Thirty-eight years later, the lamp was upgraded to a fifth-order lens. Lynde Point Light was electrified in 1955 and automated

Lynde Point Light

Also known as Saybrook Lighthouse
Old Saybrook, Connecticut

in 1978. The 1890 fifth-order Fresnel is still in operation at Lynde Point, exhibiting a fixed white beam.

The old keeper's house was demolished in 1966 and replaced with a modern duplex to house Coast Guard employees.

Directions

The lighthouse station is not accessible to the public, but it can be seen from various points in the area. *From I-95 North*: Take exit 67 to Elm Street and turn right. Cross US 1 to CT 154 (Main Street), then follow CT 154 to the left to Saybrook Point. *From I-95 South*: Take exit 69 to US 1. Continue into Old Saybrook Center on US 1/CT 154; bear left and follow CT 154 (Main Street) to Saybrook Point. From Saybrook Point, continue 0.5 mile to the South Cove Bridge and causeway. The lighthouse can be seen from this area. As you continue on CT 154, the lighthouse can be seen from several vantage points, including Knollwood Beach (1.9 miles from Saybrook Point). See Appendix for information on lighthouse cruises and charters.

Latitude: 41°16'18"N
Longitude: 72°20'36"W

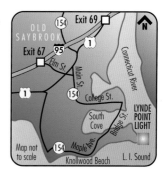

Contact Information:
U.S. Coast Guard Group/
MSO Long Island Sound
120 Woodward Avenue
New Haven, CT 06512
(800) 774-8724

Montauk Point Lighthouse

New York's first lighthouse, Montauk Point was authorized by President George Washington in 1795. John McComb Jr., who had successfully constructed a tower at Cape Henry, Virginia, was selected as the site's architect. Construction was completed on November 5, 1796, at a cost of $22,300.

Standing high on Turtle Hill, Montauk Point Lighthouse marks the easternmost point of New York and was often the first American landmark that mariners and international visitors spotted. Until the Statue of Liberty was constructed in 1886, Montauk Point Light served as an unofficial welcome to the United States.

Though the octagonal sandstone tower is the original one built in the 18th century, several changes have been made to the property. For instance, the light tower was 80 feet tall when built; it was raised to its current height of 110 feet in 1860 to accommodate the first-order Fresnel lens installed three years earlier. Other changes include construction of a new keeper's dwelling in 1860, the adoption of the current brown-and-white-striped color scheme in 1900, and the addition of a three-and-one-half order bivalve lens in 1903.

The 1857 addition of a Fresnel lens coincided with a change from the former fixed white light to a blinking light, so as not to cause confusion

Montauk Point Lighthouse

Montauk, Long Island, New York

between Montauk Point and the new fixed-white-light Shinnecock Light, located between the Fire Island and Montauk Point Lighthouses. Unfortunately, the crew of the *John Milton* was not aware of the changes. Returning home from a two-year voyage in February 1858, the captain mistook the Shinnecock Light for Montauk Point and crashed the ship into the rocky Long Island shore. All 33 passengers died.

In 1986 the U.S. Coast Guard transferred ownership of the lighthouse to the Montauk Historical Society in order to maintain and preserve the light's historical significance. A year later, the beacon was automated and a new modern optic was installed. Today the light flashes a white beam every five seconds and can be seen from a distance of 19 miles. The Montauk Historical Society runs a museum and gift shop in the tower.

Directions

To reach Montauk Point Lighthouse, travel east on I-495. From there, you may choose one of two routes. For a more scenic drive, take exit 70 off I-495 to get on Route 111 south. This will lead you to Route 27. Travel east on Route 27 until you hit Montauk Point. For a faster route, take I-495 to exit 30. Travel south on the Cross Island Parkway until you hit exit 25A. Take the exit to merge onto Southern State Parkway East. Take exit 44E (Route 27) and follow the road to Montauk Point.

Latitude: 41°04'18"N
Longitude: 71°51'24"W

Contact Information:
Montauk Historical Society
RFD # 2
Box 112
Montauk, NY 11954
(631) 668-2544
www.montauklighthouse.com

Morgan Point Lighthouse

Morgan Point Lighthouse stands at the mouth of the Mystic River on land purchased from an ancestor of James Morgan, who originally settled the area. A 25-foot circular granite tower and separate keeper's house were built here in 1831, but as the town's fishing and shipbuilding industries multiplied in the 1860s, the need for a new lighthouse became apparent.

Morgan Point Lighthouse

Noank, Connecticut

The second lighthouse at Morgan Point began operation in 1868. Among the updated aspects of the light were a combined tower and keeper's house. The new tower was equipped with the sixth-order Fresnel lens that had replaced the 10 lamps and reflectors in the previous tower in 1855. The lighthouse was discontinued in 1919 when an automatic electric light was placed at the channel entrance to the Mystic River. Morgan Point Lighthouse is now privately owned, but the Noank Historical Society has a collection of historical items from the site.

Directions

This lighthouse is privately owned and not open to the public. It is best seen from the water. (See Appendix for charter and lighthouse cruise information.)

Latitude: 41°19'00"N
Longitude: 71°59'23"W

Contact Information:
Noank Historical Society Museum
17 Sylvan Street
Noank, CT 06340
(860) 536-7026

Mystic Seaport Lighthouse

Mystic Seaport is a replica of an authentic 19th-century coastal village featuring tall ships, fisheries, and exhibits on such 19th-century activities as ropemaking, barrelmaking, and boatbuilding. In the heart of the village is a reproduction of Brant Point Light, built in 1746 on the island of Nantucket in Massachusetts. A plaque on the lighthouse in Mystic Seaport details the construction and history of the 250-year-old beacon.

The original Brant Point Light, America's third-oldest light station, was appropriated by Nantucket merchants and mariners at a town meeting in January 1746. The prosperous whaling town necessitated a beacon to help ships navigate into the town's inner harbor. Two hundred English pounds were raised to fund the lighthouse, which was constructed of wood over the next few years. Unfortunately, the light was burned to the ground in a 1757 fire.

Mystic Seaport Lighthouse

Also known as Brant Point Light (Replica)
Mystic, Connecticut

Directions

From I-95 South: Take exit 90 and turn left at end of ramp onto Route 27 South. *From I-95 North*: Take exit 90, and, from the right lane, turn right at the light onto Route 27 South. From either direction, proceed approximately 1 mile after turning onto Route 27 South. Pass North Parking lot on the left (opposite Seamen's Inne). Mystic Seaport South Parking is the second lot on your left and opposite the main entrance to the visitor center. This lot provides the easiest access point to the museum.

Latitude: N/A
Longitude: N/A

Contact Information:
Mystic Seaport
P.O. Box 6000
75 Greenmanville Avenue
Mystic, CT 06355-0990
(860) 572-0711
www.mysticseaport.org

New London Harbor Lighthouse

As New London's whaling industry began to thrive in the 18th century, the need became apparent for a lighthouse to mark the entrance to the Thames River. The 64-foot granite tower constructed here in 1760 was the fourth lighthouse built in the United States. Funds for the lighthouse's construction and upkeep were raised through a lottery and through a tonnage tax imposed on shipping. During the Revolutionary War, light from the tower's lantern helped American privateers find shelter from British warships.

By 1799 a ten-foot fracture had developed in the tower and mariners complained that the light was ineffective. A new 89-foot, octagonal-shaped lighthouse was completed in 1801 and fitted with 11 whale-oil lamps with 13-inch reflectors. Unlike the Revolutionary War, in which New London Harbor Lighthouse had played a significant role, the beacon was extinguished by Americans during the War of 1812 so the British could not navigate the harbor.

New London Harbor Lighthouse

New London, Connecticut

A new keeper's quarters was built in 1818; the present dwelling was built in 1863 and enlarged in 1900. In 1912 New London Harbor Light was automated and the detached keeper's quarters were sold at auction. Today, the tower is still an active aid to navigation with its 1857 fourth-order Fresnel shining a fixed white light with an added red sector. The keeper's quarters are privately owned, and both the tower and the keeper's quarters are closed to the public.

Directions

From I-95 North: Take exit 82A to Colman Street and turn right (exit 82B if southbound). Turn left at Bank Street, then right at Shaw Street onto connecting Pequot Avenue. The lighthouse is just south of Montauk Avenue on Pequot Avenue. You can see the lighthouse from the sidewalk; do not enter the station as it is private property. Signs on the property warn against trespassing and taking photos. The lighthouse can be clearly seen from the Fishers Island, Block Island, Montauk Point, and Orient Point ferries leaving New London. It can also be viewed from several lighthouse cruises (see Appendix).

Latitude: 41°19'00"N
Longitude: 72°05'24"W

Contact Information:
U.S. Coast Guard Group/
MSO Long Island Sound
120 Woodward Avenue
New Haven, CT 06512
(800) 774-8724

New London Ledge Lighthouse

The three-story New London Ledge Lighthouse is easily recognizable by its red brick, white trim, and French Second Empire–style architecture, elements incorporated to be in keeping with the elegant architecture of the coastal New London community. One of the last lighthouses built in New England, construction began on the lighthouse in 1906 after mariners complained of a need for a signal to warn of the 200-foot shoal where the lighthouse sits. The Hamilton R. Douglas Company of New London completed work on the lighthouse in 1909 and it was fitted with a rotating fourth-order Fresnel lens. New London Ledge Lighthouse was automated in 1987 and today the lantern's modern optic is powered by solar panels and an underwater cable.

Local legend recounts the tale of a former keeper who is said to have jumped to his death after learning his wife ran off with a ferry captain. "Ernie" is said to haunt the building today, setting off the foghorn, opening and closing doors, and untying secured boats in the area.

New London Ledge Lighthouse

New London, Connecticut

Today, New London Ledge Lighthouse is leased by the New London Ledge Lighthouse Foundation. The nonprofit group is working to restore the tower's interior and hopes to open the property as a museum and bed-and-breakfast establishment.

Directions

New London Ledge Lighthouse can be viewed from the shore of New London and also from the Fishers Island and Block Island ferries that depart from New London. Charters and lighthouse cruises are also available (see Appendix).

Latitude: 41°18'18"N
Longitude: 72°04'42"W

Contact Information:
New London Ledge
Lighthouse Foundation
P.O. Box 855
New London, CT 06320
(860) 442-2222

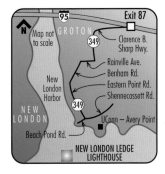

North Dumpling Light

North Dumpling Island is a two-acre island located in Fishers Island Sound. Originally owned by Native Americans, the island was sold to the Winthrop family and then to the U.S. government. Today, the island is again privately owned.

North Dumpling Island made headlines in the early 1990s when owner Dean Kamen issued a letter of secession from the United States after having been denied permission to construct a wind turbine on the property. Kamen stated in the secession letter sent to his friend, then-President George H. W. Bush, that the island was thereafter to be known as the Republic of North Dumpling and, as owner, Kamen became "Lord Dumpling." Though the secession was never officially recognized, The Republic of North Dumpling has its own official currency (one unit is the equivalent value of pi), constitution, flag, and national anthem.

The Republic of North Dumpling also has its own navy (consisting of one amphibious vehicle), a replica of Stonehenge, and the North Dumpling Light, constructed when the U.S. government owned the land in 1849.

North Dumpling Light

Fishers Island Sound, Fishers Island, New York

The tower was rebuilt from wood and brick as an octagonal, 31-foot tower attached to a wooden one-and-a-half-story French Second Empire–style keeper's dwelling in 1871. In 1959, the light's fifth-order Fresnel lens was removed from the tower and automated atop a nearby skeleton tower. After new owners extensively repaired and updated North Dumpling Light, the tower was relighted in 1980 and fitted with a modern 300-mm optic. The light is an active aid to navigation for the U.S. Coast Guard.

Directions

The lighthouse is privately owned, but it may be seen by boat; see Appendix for information on area charters and lighthouse cruises.

Latitude: 41°17'18"N
Longitude: 72°01'12"W

Contact Information:
Privately owned.

Old Field Point Lighthouse

A lighthouse marking the entrance to Port Jefferson Harbor was built in this former fishing and farming community in 1824. The original octagonal tower, built for $4,000, was 30 feet tall and detached from a one-story stone keeper's dwelling. Originally powered by nine oil lamps, the beacon was installed with a fourth-order Fresnel lens in 1855.

By 1868 maritime traffic in the harbor had increased, and a new, larger tower was constructed on the site. Comprising a 35-foot black tower atop a two-and-a-half-story Victorian Gothic Revival granite keepers' dwelling, the beacon was fitted with a fourth-order Fresnel lens.

In 1933 Old Field Point Lighthouse was deactivated and replaced by a nearby skeletal tower with an automated beacon. However, Old Field Point Lighthouse was relighted in 1991. Today, the lighthouse property is owned by the Village of Old Field. It houses town offices and serves as a residence to the town's constable. Old Field Point Lighthouse and its grounds are closed to the public, but the light continues as an active aid to navigation, alternately flashing red and green lights every 10 seconds.

Old Field Point Lighthouse

Old Field, Long Island, New York

Directions

Old Field Lighthouse is closed to the public. However, to reach the station's grounds, take Highway 25A to the town of Stony Brook. Turn north on Quaker Path Road. After about 2 miles, Quaker Path Road will merge with Old Field Road. Follow Old Field Road to the end, where you will see the lighthouse. The ferry from Port Jefferson, New York, to Bridgeport, Connecticut, also provides a view of the lighthouse.

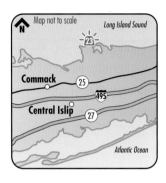

Latitude: 40°58'37"N
Longitude: 73°07'07"W

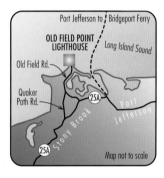

Contact Information:
Village of Old Field
Administrative Offices
(631) 941-9412
www.oldfieldny.org

Orient Point Light

Affectionately known as "the Coffee Pot," Orient Point Light was built in 1899 to mark the Oyster Pond Reef and to guide mariners through the channel known as Plum Gut that separates the north fork of Long Island from Plum Island. The sparkplug-style structure is 45 feet tall and built of iron with a brick lining.

Orient Point Light was automated in 1954. In 1970 the U.S. Coast Guard declared the light to be unfit for personnel and too expensive for repair. The light was decommissioned and slated to be demolished. Strong local protest ensued, and soon work began to restore the beacon. Three years later, Orient Point Light was reinstated as an active aid to navigation. Though the tower still suffers from a slight lean (it is five degrees out of plumb), it exhibits a flashing white light every five seconds.

In 1999 Orient Point Light celebrated its 100-year anniversary. The East End Seaport Museum and Marine Foundation, along with Coast Guard and Navy personnel, celebrated the event with a special ceremony held on a Coast Guard cutter, a helicopter fly-by, and a gun salute.

Orient Point Light

Orient Point, Long Island, New York

Directions

The Cross Sound Ferry that travels from New London, Connecticut, to Orient Point, New York, offers an excellent view of Orient Point Light. The lighthouse can also be seen from the beach at the south end of the ferry terminal and from several lighthouse cruises (see Appendix).

Latitude: 41°09'48"N
Longitude: 72°13'24"W

Contact Information:
U.S. Coast Guard Group/
MSO Long Island Sound
Aids to Navigation Team
120 Woodward Avenue
New Haven, CT 06512
(203) 468-4510
www.uscg.mil/d1/units/grumsolis/

Pecks Ledge Light

Pecks Ledge Light is situated on the east end of the Norwalk Islands. Although a light was proposed here years earlier, Pecks Ledge Light was not completed until 1906, four years after the station at nearby Greens Ledge was built. The light was designed with a cylindrical cast-iron foundation and took the form of other sparkplug-style lights in the area. Inside the lighthouse are three floors of living space, topped by a lantern fitted with a fourth-order Fresnel lens.

The lighthouse was staffed for only 27 years before being automated in 1933. Although the original lens was replaced by a modern 250-mm optic, the lighthouse continues to exhibit a flashing green light to guide mariners.

Pecks Ledge Light

Norwalk, Connecticut

Directions

This lighthouse can be viewed from Calf Pasture Park in South Norwalk. *From I-95 North*: Take exit 16 to East Avenue, turn left onto CT 136 (Cemetery Street), then follow as the road merges onto Gregory Boulevard. Follow Gregory Boulevard south through a curve to the left (around a monument) to the intersection of Fifth Street and Calf Pasture Beach Road. Turn right onto Calf Pasture Beach Road and continue to Calf Pasture Park. To your left at the entrance is a large parking area from which the lighthouse can be seen. The view is fairly distant; bring binoculars. The park is open year-round, sunrise to sunset. There is a parking fee during the summer. The lighthouse can also be seen distantly from the ferry to Sheffield Island, which departs from the Hope Dock near the Maritime Aquarium in Norwalk. Call (203) 838-9444 for more information.

Latitude: 41°04'36"N
Longitude: 73°22'12"W

Contact Information:
U.S. Coast Guard Group/
MSO Long Island Sound
120 Woodward Avenue
New Haven, CT 06512
(800) 774-8724

Penfield Reef Light

Penfield Reef Light, established on January 16, 1874, was designed by famed 19th-century lighthouse architect F. Hopkinson Smith, who also designed New York's Race Rock Light. The construction plan for the light consisted of a two-story granite house meant to serve as keeper's quarters built onto a cylindrical stone pier. A 35-foot octagonal tower sits atop the keeper's quarters and originally held a fourth-order Fresnel lens exhibiting a flashing red light every six seconds.

Legend tells that the ghost of keeper Frederick Jordan haunts the area. Jordan, who drowned while in transit to the mainland for Christmas leave in 1916, has been known to tinker with the light and save mariners in distress in stormy weather conditions.

Penfield Reef Light

Fairfield, Connecticut

In 1969 the Coast Guard announced plans to demolish the tower, but the plan was never carried out, thanks to a significant outpouring of support from local residents. Automated in 1971, Penfield Reef Light continues to serve as a navigational aid today with a modern DCB-24 aerobeacon and an automated electric horn that emits a blast every 15 seconds.

Directions

The lighthouse can be seen distantly from Fairfield Beach. From I-95 take exit 22 to Round Hill Road and turn right. Follow Round Hill Road across US 1 (Boston Post Road) onto Beach Road. Turn right at Fairfield Beach Road. Follow the road south through a zigzag intersection. A short distance from the intersection on the left is a narrow lane, across the street from College Place. Parking is not allowed on Fairfield Beach Road near the lane, so park on Reef Road or another side street. The lane to the beach is marked with LIGHTHOUSE PT. and PENFIELD REEF RIGHT OF WAY signs. Walk down the lane to the beach. The lighthouse can be seen 1.3 miles off to the southwest.

Latitude: 41°07'00"N
Longitude: 73°13'18"W

Contact Information:
U.S. Coast Guard Group/
MSO Long Island Sound
120 Woodward Avenue
New Haven, CT 06512
(800) 774-8724

Plum Island Light

Plum Island first saw the establishment of a beacon in 1827. The light warned mariners of the strong currents and dangerous shoals of Plum Gut, the waterway between Orient Point and Plum Island. At 30 feet high, the original octagonal tower was initially fitted with 10 Winslow Lewis patent lamps with 13-inch reflectors before being replaced with a fourth-order Fresnel lens in 1856.

In 1868 the lighthouse was reported to be poorly constructed—the stone was crumbling, the tower leaked, and the lantern was inefficient. The tower and keeper's quarters were demolished and a new two-story granite dwelling with an attached 55-foot cast-iron tower was built between 1869 and 1870.

Plum Island Light

Plum Island, Long Island, New York

In 1978 Plum Island Light was deactivated. Since that time, the light has stood abandoned on the island, which today is isolated as a center for animal disease research. After years of neglect, Plum Island Light has deteriorated significantly and is threatened by erosion. In 1997 the station's generator house washed away due to the encroaching shoreline.

Though riprap has been added to support the lighthouse's foundation, Plum Island Light is still in danger. East End Lighthouses, a chapter of the American Lighthouse Foundation, and the Long Island branch of the United States Lighthouse Society recently partnered in a campaign to save this historic light. The group is raising funds and assembling a team of professionals to restore the light so this critical piece of Long Island's history won't be lost.

Directions

Plum Island is closed to the public; therefore, the light can only be viewed from the water. A good view can be had from the Cross Sound Ferry that travels from New London, Connecticut, to Orient Point, New York. The East End Seaport and Marine Foundation hosts a lighthouse cruise in June that includes Plum Island Light. Contact the museum at (516) 477-2121 for more information. (See Appendix for listings of other cruises and charters).

Latitude: 41°10'26"N
Longitude: 72°12'43"W

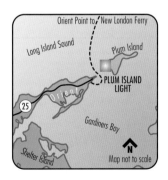

Contact Information:
East End Lighthouses
P.O. Box 21
Greenport, NY 11944
(631) 477-4121
www.eastendlighthouses.org

Race Rock Light

Race Rock Light marks a particularly treacherous area off Fishers Island known as "The Race." This area is known for its heavy currents in both directions, depending on the tide, and particularly dangerous waves during stormy conditions. Hundreds of shipwrecks have occurred here—eight vessels were wrecked between 1829 and 1837 alone. After unsuccessfully attempting to mark the area with buoys in 1847 and an iron spindle in 1853, Congress appropriated $90,000 to construct a light station on Race Rock.

The station, built by designer Francis Hopkinson Smith and architect Captain Thomas Scott, became notorious for its lengthy and costly construction process—it took eight years to complete at an outlandish final cost of $278,716. The delays were blamed on bad weather, strong currents, and mismanagement.

Race Rock Light

Fishers Island, Long Island, New York

Race Rock Light stands on an underwater ledge, and the laying and leveling of the foundation took a great deal of time and material. Ten thousand tons of granite were used in the riprap foundation, and divers had to assist with leveling the ledge with small pieces of stone.

Construction was completed on the 45-foot square granite tower and one-and-a-half story Gothic Revival–style keeper's quarters in 1878. The tower was installed with a fourth-order Fresnel lens that was first lighted on January 1, 1879. In 1896, a second-class fog siren replaced the previous machine-operated fog bell.

The long efforts of the construction crew paid off, as the original buildings have remained in good condition throughout the past 125 years. In 1978 Race Rock Light was automated, and a modern optic now shines alternating red and white flashes every 30 seconds.

Directions

Race Rock Light can only be viewed by boat. Several charters and tours pass Race Rock Light in their travels (see Appendix).

Latitude: 41°14'36"N
Longitude: 72°02'48"W

Contact Information:
U.S. Coast Guard Group/
MSO Long Island Sound
Aids to Navigation Team
120 Woodward Avenue
New Haven, CT 06512
(203) 468-4510
www.uscg.mil/d1/units/grumsolis/

Sands Point Lighthouse

Sands Point Lighthouse was established in 1809. It is sometimes called Mitchell Lighthouse after Samuel Mitchell, who in 1790 recommended that a station be constructed on Sands Point, located at the tip of the Port Washington peninsula.

A 65-foot stone octagonal tower and two-and-a-half story colonial-style keeper's dwelling (added to the tower in 1868) comprise the station at Sands Point. Noah Mason, a Revolutionary War veteran who helped build the lighthouse, served as Sands Point's first keeper. Eleven lamps with nine-inch reflectors originally outfitted the lantern room; however, these were replaced in 1856 by a fourth-order Fresnel lens.

In December 1922, Sands Point Light was deactivated and later sold at auction. In 1927, the property was purchased by William Randolph Hearst, who reportedly held grandiose parties at the lighthouse.

Sands Points is inactive and privately owned. A nearby skeletal light warns mariners of the approaching shoreline.

Sands Point Lighthouse

Also known as Mitchell Lighthouse
Port Washington, Long Island, New York

Directions

Sands Point Lighthouse is private property and not accessible to the public. It is best viewed by boat.

Latitude: 40°51'57"N
Longitude: 73°43'46"W

Contact Information:
Privately owned.

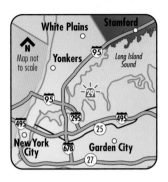

Saybrook Breakwater Lighthouse

In 1886, Saybrook Breakwater Light, commonly known as the "Outer Light," was built 1.5 miles from Lynde Point Light to assist in marking a sandbar at the entrance of the mouth of the Connecticut River. The 49-foot cast-iron tower stands on a concrete foundation and consists of a basement, four main floors, a watch deck, and a lantern room.

Saybrook Breakwater Lighthouse

Old Saybrook, Connecticut

A 1,000-pound fog bell was installed at the light station in 1889, but after complaints about the noise from local residents, the bell was replaced with a 250-pound alternate. This was eventually replaced by the two foghorns that currently sound every 30 seconds. Likewise, the 17 lamps and fifth-order Fresnel that originally fitted the lighthouse were replaced with a fourth-order lens in 1890. Automated in 1959, a modern optic at Saybrook Breakwater Lighthouse continues to flash green every six seconds.

Since 1993, Saybrook Breakwater Lighthouse has adorned Connecticut's "Preserve the Sound" license plates, the proceeds from which go to the Long Island Sound Fund. Through this fund, the Department of Environmental Protection distributes grant money to schools, municipalities, and nonprofit groups that work to preserve the Sound and increase public awareness of its importance.

Directions

Saybrook Breakwater Light can be seen from points on CT 154 in Old Saybrook, but it is best viewed from the water. See Appendix for charter and cruise information.

Latitude: 41°15'48"N
Longitude: 72°20'36"W

Contact Information:
U.S. Coast Guard Group/
MSO Long Island Sound
120 Woodward Avenue
New Haven, CT 06512
(800) 774-8724

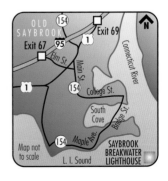

Sheffield Island Light

Originally known as White Island, Sheffield Island was renamed as such when Robert Sheffield purchased the 53-acre property off the coast of Norwalk in 1804. Twenty-two years later, Sheffield's son-in-law sold four acres of the island to the U.S. government for the purpose of establishing a light station. Sheffield Island Light was first lit in 1828. The original station had a small stone keeper's house and an unusual lighting system that consisted of 10 lamps and reflectors, powered by a rotating clockwork mechanism that flashed alternating red and white lights. In 1857 that system was replaced with a fourth-order Fresnel lens.

This lighthouse was replaced in 1868 with a 44-foot stone Victorian-style building. In 1902, after the construction of Greens Ledge Light to the west, Sheffield Island Light was deactivated. The tower and property were sold at auction in 1914 for less than $5,000 to a private owner. The tower remained

Sheffield Island Light

Norwalk, Connecticut

in private hands until 1986, when it was sold to the Norwalk Seaport Organization. The group has since completely restored the lighthouse and taken steps to prevent further erosion to the property. Sheffield Island Light is open to the public as a museum; the Norwalk Seaport Association provides a ferry that travels to the island daily throughout the summer.

Directions

To visit Sheffield Island, you must board a ferry from the Hope Dock. *From I-95 North*: Take exit 14N and follow Fairfield Avenue and Reed Street to West Avenue. Turn right onto West Avenue. At the West Avenue–M. L. King–North Main Street intersection, bear left onto North Main Street. Turn left at Ann Street, then continue to North Water Street and a municipal parking lot where all-day parking is available for a fee. Parking tickets can be validated at the Maritime Aquarium. The Hope Dock is next to the Aquarium. *From I-95 South*: Take exit 15S and bear right at the fork. At the bottom of the ramp, turn left at West Avenue. From there the directions are the same as from I-95 North.

Latitude: 41°02'56"N
Longitude: 73°25'09"W

Contact Information:
Norwalk Seaport Association
132 Water Street
South Norwalk, CT 06854
(203) 838-9444
www.seaport.org

Southwest Ledge Light

Southwest Ledge Light is built on a dangerous rock formation that sits approximately 1 mile from New Haven Harbor. While it was recommended that a light be built here in 1845, the government's budget did not allow for construction until 1877. The lighthouse represented the latest in technology, featuring a cylindrical iron structure and foundation, Mansard roofing,

Southwest Ledge Light

Also known as New Haven Breakwater Light
New Haven, Connecticut

and an octagonal lantern room. In fact, a model of the superstructure was displayed at the 1876 Centennial Exposition in Philadelphia, where an actual lighthouse keeper maintained a light in the tower throughout the show. This model later became Ship John Shoal Light, stationed in Delaware. Due to its optimum performance, Southwest Ledge Light put nearby New Haven Harbor Light out of commission upon its activation.

A fourth-order Fresnel lens was installed in the new beacon and a fog signal followed a few years later. Poor conditions at the lighthouse, including leaky walls, undrinkable water, and an infestation of cockroaches, led to a high keeper turnover rate over the years. Finally, the light was automated in 1973. With the help of a modern lens installed in 1988, the lighthouse continues to serve mariners today.

Directions

Southwest Ledge Light can be seen distantly from Lighthouse Point Park in New Haven. *From I-95 North:* Take exit 50N (from I-95 South, take exit 51S) to Townsend Avenue. Follow to Lighthouse Road and turn right to the park entrance.

Latitude: 41°14'06"N
Longitude: 72°54'42"W

Contact Information:
U.S. Coast Guard Group/
MSO Long Island Sound
120 Woodward Avenue
New Haven, CT 06512
(800) 774-8724

Stamford Harbor Light

Although stationed off the shore of Connecticut, Stamford Harbor Light was built in Boston. After the various sections of the 60-foot sparkplug-style cast-iron tower were constructed, they were transported to Chatham Rock, where the finished tower was assembled on a cylindrical pier.

The lighthouse, fitted with a fourth-order Fresnel lens and equipped with a fog bell, went into service in 1882. It remained in service for more than 80 years but was eventually deactivated in 1953 and replaced by a nearby skeletal tower. The lighthouse was then placed for sale, but it was two years before the property was finally purchased for the astounding price of $1.00. Stamford Harbor Light has had a series of private owners over the last five

Stamford Harbor Light

Also known as Chatham Rocks Light
Stamford, Connecticut

decades and underwent extensive renovation in the 1980s. In the mid-1990s Stamford Harbor Light was placed for sale with an asking price of $1.1 million. However, the lighthouse has since been removed from the market.

Directions

The lighthouse can be seen from the Shippan Point section of Stamford. *From I-95*: Take exit 8 to Elm Street. Turn right at Jefferson Street, then left at Magee Street, and continue straight through an intersection where it becomes Shippan Street. Turn right at Ocean Drive, then right at Fairview Avenue. Park on the side of Fairview Avenue and walk down to the small beach at its dead end. The lighthouse can be seen near the West Breakwater. It may also be possible to see the lighthouse from some lighthouse cruises (see Appendix).

Latitude: 41°00'54"N
Longitude: 73°32'18"W

**Contact Information:
Privately owned.**

Stepping Stones Lighthouse

This area northwest of Elm Point in Great Neck gets its name from an ancient Native American legend. According to the tale, the Siwanoy Indians were battling the devil for possession of the land now known as Connecticut and had pushed the devil back to Long Island Sound. The devil used a series of boulders in the Sound to leap across and escape from the attacking Siwanoy. Early maps of the area refer to the Sound as "Devil's Belt," and the Sound's reefs are referred to as the "Devil's Stepping Stones."

The lighthouse here was originally intended for Hart Island, but the government was unable to obtain the land needed. In 1874, the decision was made to change the location to Stepping Stones, which lies about 1,600 yards offshore, and construction began a year later.

Stepping Stones Lighthouse

Kings Point, Long Island, New York

On March 1, 1877, keeper Findlay Fraser lit Stepping Stones Lighthouse for the first time. The 38-foot red brick Second Empire–style tower was originally fitted with a fifth-order Fresnel lens that exhibited a fixed red light, but was upgraded to a fourth-order Fresnel with a fixed green light in 1932.

Stepping Stones Lighthouse was automated in 1967 and serves as an active aid to navigation, though a modern optic now services the beacon.

Directions

Stepping Stones Lighthouse is best viewed from the water. However, it can also be seen from the Throgs Neck Bridge on Interstate 295 or the south end of City Island, New York.

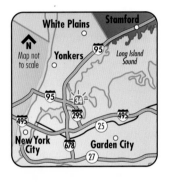

Latitude: 40°49'30"N
Longitude: 73°46'30"W

Contact Information:
U.S. Coast Guard Group/
MSO Long Island Sound
Aids to Navigation Team
120 Woodward Avenue
New Haven, CT 06512
(203) 468-4510
www.uscg.mil/d1/units/grumsolis/

Stonington Harbor Lighthouse

Stonington Harbor Lighthouse was established in 1824 to help whaling and fishing ships navigate Fishers Island Sound and Stonington Harbor. The first tower was built at the end of the mile-long peninsula known as Stonington Borough. It consisted of a small keeper's house and a 30-foot granite tower that housed a lantern containing 10 oil lamps and parabolic reflectors. Upon inspection in 1838, it was discovered that erosion threatened to destroy the lighthouse. In addition, the silver coating on the reflectors had been worn thin from polishing, and the tower's wooden stairway was deteriorating quickly. Rather than spending the time and money to repair the lighthouse, the federal government made the decision to replace the building.

The current 35-foot granite tower and keeper's house were built in 1840. In 1856 a sixth-order Fresnel lens replaced the former system of eight lamps and a series of reflectors. Although the light was discontinued upon construction of the Stonington Breakwater Light in 1889, Stonington Harbor Lighthouse was purchased by the Stonington Historical Society in 1925 and today serves as a museum honoring the rich history of the area.

Stonington Harbor Lighthouse

Directions

Take exit 91 off I-95 and turn south on Route 234 (Pequot Trail). Continue 0.4 mile to North Main Street. Turn left on North Main and follow 1.5 miles to a light at the intersection with Route 1. Cross Route 1 and continue straight to a stop sign. Turn left and then take the next right over the railroad bridge to Water Street. Follow Water Street through historic Stonington Village to the end. Park at the Point and walk up to the lighthouse. The lighthouse can also be viewed from the water. See Appendix for cruise and charter information.

Latitude: 41°19'43"N
Longitude: 71°54'20"W

Contact Information:
Stonington Historical Society
P.O. Box 103
Stonington, CT 06378
(860) 535-1440
www.stoningtonhistory.org/light.htm

Stratford Point Lighthouse

Stratford Point Lighthouse was built in 1822 to warn mariners of the shifting sandbars, rugged cliffs, and strong currents at the mouth of the Housatonic River. Before the light was built, a bonfire and then an iron basket on a pole were used as navigational aids at this location.

The light station was equipped with a fog bell in 1864. Since this location is prone to fog, the bell received a lot of use. Legend has it that one keeper rang the fog bell for 104 consecutive hours during a February storm, stopping for only a brief rest before continuing to ring the bell for another 103 hours.

A cone-shaped, cast-iron, brick-lined tower and eight-room Gothic Revival–style keeper's quarters replaced the original octagonal wooden structure in 1881. The 35-foot tower is painted white with a red band in the middle and originally held a third-order Fresnel lens. In 1906 the third-order Fresnel was replaced with a fourth-order lens, which in turn was removed in 1969 to

Stratford, Connecticut

make way for the most powerful lighting system of any Connecticut light-house—a system of DCB-224 rotating lights. The fourth-order Fresnel was placed on display at Stratford's Boothe Memorial Park, where it remained for more than 20 years. In 1990, however, the lantern was reinstalled and the aerobeacons were replaced with a 190-millimeter modern optic, the lighting system that stands intact today.

Today, the keeper's quarters are home to a Coast Guard family, and the light station and its property are closed to the public.

Directions

The keeper's house is used as Coast Guard housing; there is no public access. The lighthouse is best viewed from the water.

Latitude: 41°09'06"N
Longitude: 73°06'12"W

Contact Information:
U.S. Coast Guard Group/
MSO Long Island Sound
120 Woodward Avenue
New Haven, CT 06512
(800) 774-8724

Stratford Shoal Light

Although many navigational aids, including fixed-spar buoys and a lightship, were used at Stratford Shoal in earlier centuries, the Lighthouse Board called for the establishment of a permanent fixture in 1872. One of the last granite island lighthouses built, Stratford Shoal Light became operational in December 1877. The lighthouse, originally equipped with a fourth-order Fresnel, stands 35 feet high, and its flashing white light is visible from 60 feet above sea level.

In 1879 a fog bell was added to the building. It was replaced several times over the years, and the light presently houses an automatic fog signal that emits one blast every 15 seconds. Likewise, Stratford Shoal Light's Fresnel lens was replaced several times over the years—by fourth-order Fresnels in 1894 and 1905, by a 300-millimeter optic in 1988, and, most recently, by the 190-millimeter solar-powered lens that continues to power the light today. Stratford Shoal Light has been automated since 1970.

Stratford Shoal Light

Also known as Middleground Light
Bridgeport, Connecticut

Directions

Stratford Shoal Light is best seen by private boat, but it can be seen distantly from the Bridgeport-Port Jefferson (New York) Ferry. Call (203) 367-3043 for information. The ferry carries passengers and cars year-round, and there are frequent departures from both ports.

Latitude: 41°03'36"N
Longitude: 73°06'06"W

Contact Information:
U.S. Coast Guard Group/
MSO Long Island Sound
120 Woodward Avenue
New Haven, CT 06512
(800) 774-8724

Tongue Point Light

Tongue Point Light, notable because of its black paint scheme, marks an 11,000-foot breakwater built in Bridgeport Harbor. The 31-foot cast-iron lighthouse, built in 1895, was installed with a sixth-order Fresnel lens exhibiting a fixed white light. Just a few years later, Tongue Point Light was selected for testing of a new electric-powered fog bell. The device proved to be unsatisfactory, and a standard fog bell was issued to replace the experimental apparatus.

No keeper's quarters were built at Tongue Point Light; rather, the duties of looking after the structure were given to the keeper of Bridgeport Harbor Light, Stephen McNeil. Not surprisingly, the double burden left McNeil ragged, and he hired an assistant to tend to Bridgeport Harbor Light while

Tongue Point Light

Also known as Bridgeport Breakwater Light
Bridgeport, Connecticut

he kept watch at Tongue Point Light. A 1901 inspection found that Bridge-port Harbor Light was in poor condition, causing the Lighthouse Board to learn of McNeil's unauthorized assistant. As a result, McNeil was given the sole responsibility of looking after Tongue Point Light. He built a small shack near the lighthouse where he stayed to carry out his duties for the length of his life. After his death in 1904, McNeil's widow took over the responsibilities of Tongue Point Light, becoming the station's only female keeper.

In 1920, the shipping channel at Bridgeport Harbor was widened, necessitating a shorter breakwater. Because of this, Tongue Point Light was relocated 275 feet inland. The lighthouse was automated in 1954 and continues to serve as an active aid to navigation, exhibiting a green flash from its modern 155-millimeter optic every four seconds.

Tongue Point Light sits on land that is currently owned by a utility company. It is not accessible to the public and can be seen only by boat.

Directions

Tongue Point Lighthouse is on the grounds of a large power station; the grounds are not open to the public. A close view of this lighthouse is available from the Bridgeport-Port Jefferson (New York) Ferry. Call (203) 367-3043 for information. The ferry carries passengers and cars year-round with frequent departures from both ports.

Latitude: 41°10'00"N
Longitude: 73°10'42"W

Contact Information:
U.S. Coast Guard Group/
MSO Long Island Sound
120 Woodward Avenue
New Haven, CT 06512
(800) 774-8724

Appendix

EDITOR'S NOTE: The following information was confirmed at press time. We recommend, however, that you call the appropriate numbers to confirm lodging, attraction, and event information before traveling.

Connecticut Events

February   Connecticut Flower & Garden Show, Hartford (860-844-8461, www.ctflowershow.com)

April   Daffodil Festival, Meriden (203-630-4279, www.daffodilfest.com)

May   Lobsterfest, Mystic (888-973-2767, www.mysticseaport.org)
Meet the Artists and Artisans, Milford (features lots of lighthouse art, 203-874-5672, www.artistsandartisans.bizland.com)

June   Farmington Antiques Weekend, Farmington (317-598-0012, www.farmington-antiques.com)
International Festival of Arts & Ideas, New Haven (888-ART-IDEA, www.artidea.org)

July   Antique & Classic Boat Rendezvous, Mystic (888-973-2767, www.mysticseaport.org)
Great Connecticut Traditional Jazz Festival, Moodus (860-267-0601, www.ctjazz.org)
Guilford Handcrafts Exposition, Guilford (203-453-5947, www.handcraftcenter.org)
Independence Day at Mystic Seaport, Mystic (888-973-2767, www.mysticseaport.org)
Mashantucket Pequot Thames River Fireworks, Groton/New London (860-396-6572)
Meet the Artists and Artisans, Mystic (203-874-5672, www.artistsandartisans.bizland.com)
Riverfest, Hartford/East Hartford (860-713-3131, www.riverfront.org)
Sailfest, New London (860-444-1879, www.sailfest.org)
Subfest, Groton (860-694-3238)

August   Buick Championship PGA Event, Cromwell (860-522-4171, information; 888-BUICK-44, tickets; www.buickchampionship.com)
Litchfield Jazz Festival, Goshen (860-567-4162, www.litchfieldjazzfestival.com)
Milford Oyster Festival, Milford (203-878-5363, www.milfordoysterfestival.org)
Mystic Outdoor Art Festival, Mystic (860-572-5098, www.mysticchamber.org/mypages/moaf_sp.html)

Pilot Pen Tennis Women's Championships, New Haven (888-99-PILOT, www.pilotpentennis.com)

September   Berlin Fair, Berlin (877-828-0063, www.ctberlinfair.com)
Bethlehem Fair, Bethlehem (203-266-5350,
    www.bethlehemfair.com)
Boats, Books & Brushes, New London (888-766-BBBT,
    www.boatsbooksandbrushes.com)
Durham Fair, Durham (860-349-9495, www.durhamfair.com)
Farmington Antiques Weekend, Farmington (317-598-0012,
    www.farmingtonantiques.com)
Meet the Artists and Artisans, Milford (203-874-5672,
    www.artistsandartisans.bizland.com)
Norwalk Oyster Festival, East Norwalk (203-838-9444,
    www.seaport.org)
Woodstock Fair, South Woodstock (860-928-3246,
    www.woodstockfair.com)

October   Apple Harvest Festival, Southington (860-276-8461,
    www.appleharvestfestival.com)
Berlin Fair, Berlin (877-828-0063, www.ctberlinfair.com)
Greater Hartford Marathon, Hartford (860-652-8866,
    www.hartfordmarathon.com)
Sea Harvest, Mystic (888-973-2767, www.mysticseaport.org)
Walking Weekend, Northeast Connecticut (888-628-1228)

November   Holiday Light Fantasia, Hartford (860-343-1565,
    www.holidaylightfantasia.com)
Manchester Road Race, Manchester (860-649-6456,
    www.manchesterroadrace.com)
Stamford Parade Spectacular, Stamford (203-348-5285,
    www.stamford-downtown.com)
Wesleyan Potters Show & Sale, Middletown (860-347-5925,
    www.wesleyanpotters.com)

December   First Night Hartford, Hartford (860-722-9546,
    www.firstnighthartford.com)
Holiday Craft Exhibition and Sale, Brookfield (203-775-4526,
    www.brookfieldcraftcenter.org)
Lantern Light Tours, Mystic (888-973-2767,
    www.mysticseaport.org)

Long Island Events

February   Black History Month, Long Island State Parks (631-669-1000,
    http://nysparks.state.ny.us/)

March	St Patrick's Day Parade, Montauk (631-668-2428, www.montaukchamber.com)
May	Long Island Artists Exhibition, Huntington (631-351-3250, www.huntingtonarts.org)
	Long Island Lighthouse Challenge, Long Island (631-951-3900, www.lilighthousesociety.org)
	Long Island Marathon, Long Island (516-572-0248, www.thelimarathon.com)
	Town of Huntington Annual Tulip Festival, Huntington Village (631-271-8423, http://town.huntington.ny.us/)
June	Annual Blessing of the Fleet, Montauk (631-668-2428, www.montaukchamber.com)
	Belmont Stakes, Belmont (516-488-6000, www.nyra.com/belmont)
	Mighty Montauk Triathalon, Montauk (631-668-2428, www.montaukchamber.com)
	Summer Arts Festival, Huntington (631-271-8423, www.huntingtonarts.org)
July	Long Island Summer Festival, Oyster Bay (516-922-0061, www.fotapresents.org)
	Montauk Point Lighthouse Sprint Triathlon & Relay, Montauk (516-739-7223, www.longislandtricoach.com)
August	Lighthouse Weekend, Montauk (631-668-2544, www.montauklighthouse.com)
September	American Music Festival, Port Jefferson (631-473-4778, www.portjeff.com)
	Outdoor Art Show, Port Jefferson (631-751-7272, www.portjeff.com)
	Shinnecock Pow Wow, Southampton (631-283-6143, www.shinnecocknation.com)
October	Hamptons International Film Festival, The Hamptons (631-324-4600, www.hamptonsfilmfest.org)
	Long Island Fall Festival, Huntington Village (631-351-1910, www.lifallfestival.com)
	Mid Island Dahlia Society Flower Show, Oyster Bay (516-922-9200, www.plantingfields.org)
	Montauk Fall Festival, Montauk (631-668-2428, www.montaukchamber.com)
December	Charles Dickens Festival, Port Jefferson (631-473-1414, www.portjeff.com)
	First Night Greenport, Greenport (631-477-1383, www.greenport.cc)
	Orient Beach State Park Holiday Tree Lighting Ceremony, Orient Beach (631-323-2440)

Connecticut Lodging and Other Sites of Interest

Bridgeport (Fayerweather Island, Tongue Point Lights)
Other Sites of Interest:
The Barnum Museum (203-331-1104, www.barnum-museum.org)
Beardsley Zoo (203-394-6565, www.beardsleyzoo.org)
Captain's Cove Seaport (203-335-1433, www.captainscoveseaport.com)
The Discovery Museum (203-372-3521, www.discoverymuseum.org)
Housatonic Museum of Art (203-332-5052)

Lodging:
Holiday Inn Bridgeport (203-334-1234, www.holidayinnbridgeport.com)

Fairfield (Penfield Reef Light)
Other Sites of Interest:
Connecticut Audubon Birdcraft Museum (203-259-0416)
Connecticut Audubon Society Center at Fairfield (203-259-6305)
Ogden House and Gardens (203-259-1598, www.fairfieldhistoricalsociety.org)
Thomas J. Walsh Art Gallery at Fairfield University (203-254-4000)

Lodging:
Fairfield Inn (800-347-0414)
Merritt Parkway Motor Inn (203-259-5264)
Seagrape Inn (203-255-6808, www.seagrapeinn.com)

Greenwich (Great Captain Island Light)
Other Sites of Interest:
Audubon Center Greenwich (203-869-5272, http://greenwich.center.audubon.org)
Bruce Museum of Arts & Science (203-869-0376, www.brucemuseum.org)
Bush-Holley Historic Site & Visitor Center (203-869-6899, www.hstg.org)
Putnam Cottage (203-869-9697, www.putnamcottage.org)

Lodging:
Cos Cob Inn, Cos Cob (203-661-5845, www.coscobinn.com)
DELAMAR Greenwich Harbor, Greenwich (866-335-2627, www.thedelamar.com)
Hyatt Regency Greenwich, Greenwich (203-637-1234, www.greenwich.hyatt.com)
Stanton House Inn, Greenwich (203-869-2110, www.shinngreenwich.com)

Groton (Avery Point Light)
Other Sites of Interest:
Fort Griswold Battlefield State Park (860-444-7591)
Historic Ship Nautilus and Submarine Force Museum (800-343-0079,
    www.ussnautilus.org)
U.S. Submarine World War II Veteran's Memorial (East) (860-399-8666)

Lodging:
Benham Motel (860-449-5700)
Bestway Inn and Suites (800-280-0054)

Groton (Avery Point Light) *cont.*
Clarion Inn (866-254-0637)
Mystic Marriott Hotel & Spa (866-449-7390)
Thames Inn and Marina (860-445-8111)

Guilford (Faulkners Island Light)
Other Sites of Interest:
Dudley Farm, Guilford (203-457-0770)
Hammonasset Beach State Park, Madison (203-245-2785)
Henry Whitfield State Museum, Guilford (203-453-2457)
The Sculpture Mile, Madison (860-767-2624)
Thomas Griswold House, Guilford (203-453-3176, www.thomasgriswoldhouse.com)

Lodging:
The B&B at Bartlett Farm, Guilford (203-457-2657, www.thebartlettfarm.com)
Griswold Cottage, Guilford (203-453-1488, www.griswoldcottage.com)
Guilford Suites Hotel, Guilford (203-453-0123)
Madison Beach Hotel, Madison (203-245-1404, www.madisonbeachhotel.com)
Tidewater Inn B&B, Madison (203-245-8457, www.thetidewater.com)
Tower Suites Motel, Guilford (203-453-9069)

Mystic/Noank (Morgan Point, Mystic Seaport Lights)
Other Sites of Interest:
Denison Homestead Museum/Pequotsepos Manor, Mystic (860-536-9248)
Haight Winery, Mystic (860-572-1978)
Mystic Aquarium and Institute for Exploration, Mystic (860-572-5955,
    www.mysticaquarium.org)
Mystic Seaport, Mystic (888-973-2767, www.mysticseaport.org)
Olde Mistick Village, Mystic (860-536-4941, www.oldmysticvillage.com)

Lodging:
Adams House of Mystic, Mystic (860-572-9551, www.adamshouseofmystic.com)
Comfort Inn of Mystic, Mystic (800-572-3993)
Harbour Inne & Cottage, Mystic (860-572-9253, www.harbourinne-cottage.com)
Inn at Mystic, Mystic (800-237-2415, www.innatmystic.com)
Whitehall Mansion, Mystic (860-572-7280)

New Haven (Five Mile Point, Southwest Ledge Lights)
Other Sites of Interest:
Connecticut Children's Museum (203-562-5437, www.childrensbuilding.org)
Edgewood Park (203-946-6086)
Knights of Columbus Museum (203-865-0400)
Peabody Museum of Natural History (203-432-5050, www.peabody.yale.edu)
Yale University Visitor Information Center (203-432-2300, www.yale.edu/visitor)

Lodging:
Colony Inn (800-458-8810, www.colonyatyale.com)
The Inn at Oyster Point (86-OYSTERPT, www.oysterpointinn.com)
New Haven Hotel (800-NH-HOTEL, www.newhavenhotel.com)

Swan Cove B&B (203-776-3240, www.swancove.com)
Touch of Ireland Guest House (866-787-7990, www.touchofirelandguesthouse.com)

New London (New London Harbor, New London Ledge Lights)
Other Sites of Interest:
Connecticut College Arboretum (860-439-5020)
DNA EpiCenter (860-442-0391, www.science-epicenter.org)
Lyman Allyn Art Museum (860-443-2545, www.lymanallyn.org)
Monte Cristo Cottage (860-443-5378)
U.S. Coast Guard Academy (800-883-USCG, www.cga.edu)

Lodging:
Holiday Inn (860-442-0631)
Lighthouse Inn (888-443-8411, www.lighthouseinn-ct.com)
Queen Anne Inn (800-347-8818, www.queen-anne.com)
Radisson New London (800-333-3333)
Red Roof Inn (860-444-0001)

Norwalk (Greens Ledge, Pecks Ledge, Sheffield Island Lights)
Other Sites of Interest:
Connecticut GraphicArts Center (203-899-7999)
Lockwood-Mathews Mansion Museum (203-838-9799,
    www.lockwoodmathewsmansion.org)
The Maritime Aquarium at Norwalk (203-852-0700, www.maritimeaquarium.org)
Stepping Stones Museum for Children (203-899-0606,
    www.steppingstonesmuseum.org)
WPA Murals (203-866-0202)

Lodging:
Courtyard by Marriott (800-647-7578)
Four Points by Sheraton (203-849-9828)
Hilton Garden Inn (203-523-4000)
Homestead Studio Suites Hotel (203-847-6888)
Silvermine Tavern (888-693-9967, www.silverminetavern.com)

Old Saybrook (Lynde Point, Saybrook Point Lights)
Other Sites of Interest:
Florence Griswold Museum, Old Lyme (860-434-5542, www.flogris.org)
Fort Saybrook Monument Park, Old Saybrook (860-395-3123)
General William Hart House, Old Saybrook (860-395-1635)
Military Historians Museum, Westbrook (860-399-9460)
Westbrook Factory Outlets, Westbrook (860-399-8656)

Lodging:
Beach Plum Inn, Westbrook (860-399-9345, www.thebeachplum.com)
Bee & Thistle Inn, Old Lyme (800-622-4946, www.beeandthistleinn.com)
Captain Stannard House, Westbrook (860-399-4634, www.stannardhouse.com)
Deacon Timothy Pratt House, Old Saybrook (800-640-1195, www.pratthouse.net)
Liberty Inn, Old Saybrook (860-388-1777)

Old Saybrook (Lynde Point, Saybrook Point Lights) *cont.*
Saybrook Point Inn and Spa, Old Saybrook (800-243-0212, www.saybrook.com)

Stamford (Stamford Harbor Light)
Other Sites of Interest:
Bartlett Arboretum, Stamford (203-322-6971, http://bartlett.arboretum.uconn.edu)
Bruce Museum of Arts & Science, Greenwich (203-869-0376, www.brucemuseum.org)
Stamford Museum & Nature Center, Stamford (203-322-1646,
    www.stamfordmuseum.org)
United House Wrecking Company Antiques, Stamford (203-348-5371,
    www.unitedhousewrecking.com)

Lodging:
Courtyard by Marriott Stamford (203-358-8822)
Holiday Inn Select (203-358-8400)
Rodeway Inn Stamford (800-228-2000)
Sheraton Stamford Hotel (203-359-1300)
Stamford Suites Hotel (203-359-7300)
The Westin Stamford (203-967-2222)

Stonington (Stonington Light)
Other Sites of Interest:
Captain Nathaniel B. Palmer House, Stonington (860-535-8445)
Jonathan Edwards Winery, North Stonington (860-535-0202,
    www.jonathanedwardswinery.com)
Maple Breeze Amusement Park, Pawcatuck (860-599-1232)
Stonington Vineyards, Stonington (800-421-WINE, www.stoningtonvineyards.com)

Lodging:
Antiques & Accommodations, North Stonington (800-554-7829,
    www.antiquesandaccommodations.com)
Cove Ledge Inn & Marina, Pawcatuck (860-599-4130, www.coveledgeinn.com)
Inn at Lower Farm, North Stonington (866-535-9075, www.lowerfarm.com)
The John York House B&B, North Stonington (860-599-3075)
Stonington Motel, Stonington (860-599-2330, www.stoningtonmotel.com)

Stratford (Stratford Point, Stratford Shoal Lights)
Other Sites of Interest:
Boothe Memorial Park & Museum, Stratford (203-381-2046)
Connecticut Audubon Society Coastal Center, Milford (203-878-7440)
The Children's Garbage Museum, Stratford (203-381-9571)
Stratford Antique Center, Stratford (203-378-7754, www.stratfordantique.com)

Lodging:
Marnick's Restaurant-Motel, Stratford (203-377-6288)
Mayflower Motel, Milford (888-880-6854)
Nathan Booth House B&B, Stratford (203-378-6489)
Trumbull Marriott, Trumbull (203-378-1400)

Long Island Lodging and Other Sites of Interest

Brookhaven (Old Field Point Light)
Other Sites of Interest:
Fun4All, Inc., Port Jefferson Station (631-331-9000, www.fun4all-ny.com)
Long Island Museum of American Art, History and Carriages, Stony Brook
 (631-751-0066, www.longislandmuseum.org)
Martha Jefferson Bay Cruises, Inc., Port Jefferson (631-331-3333,
 www.marthajefferson.com)

Lodging:
Danfords on the Sound, Port Jefferson (631-928-5200, www.danfords.com)
Holly Berry Bed and Breakfast, Port Jefferson (631-331-3123,
 www.hollyberrybandb.com)
Miss Scarlett's Bed and Breakfast, Port Jefferson (631-928-5064)
The New Heritage Inn, Port Jefferson (631-473-2499, www.portjeffheritageinn.com)
White House on High Street Bed and Breakfast, Port Jefferson (631-434-1818,
 www.whitehousebb-portjefferson.com)

Fire Island (Fire Island Light)
Other Sites of Interest:
The Long Island Aquarium, Bay Shore (631-665-4600, www.liaquarium.org)
South Bay Paddlewheel Cruises, Bay Shore (631-321-9005)

Lodging:
Bay Shore Inn, Bay Shore (631-666-7275)
Econo Lodge, Bay Shore (631-666-6000, www.econolodge.com)
Sayville Motor Lodge, Sayville (631-589-7000)

Huntington (Eaton's Neck, Huntington Harbor Lights)
Other Sites of Interest:
Cold Spring Harbor Whaling Museum, Cold Spring Harbor (631-367-3418,
 www.cshwhalingmuseum.org)
Heckscher Museum of Art, Huntington (631-351-3250, www.heckscher.org)
The Suffolk County Vanderbilt Museum, Centerport (631-854-5579,
 www.vanderbiltmuseum.org)
Walt Whitman Birthplace State Historic Site and Interpretive Center, Huntington
 Station (631-427-5240, www.waltwhitman.org)

Lodging:
Centerport Harbor Bed and Breakfast, Centerport (631-754-1730)
Eastern Star, The Cruising Country Inn, East Northport (800-445-5942)
Swan View Manor, Cold Spring Harbor (631-367-2070, www.swanview.com)

North Hempstead (Execution Rocks, Sands Point, Stepping Stones Lights)
Other Sites of Interest:
Hempstead Harbor Beach Park, Port Washington (516-571-7930)

North Hempstead (Execution Rocks, Sands Point, Stepping Stones Lights) *cont.*
Holocaust Memorial and Educational Center of Nassau County,
     Glen Cove (516-571-8040)
Nassau County Museum of Art, Roslyn Harbor (516-484-9338,
     www.nassaumuseum.com)

Lodging:
The Andrew Hotel, Great Neck (516-482-2900, www.andrewhotel.com)
Harrison Conference Center, Glen Cove (516-671-6400,
     www.harrisonglencove.com)
Inn at Great Neck Hotel, Great Neck (516-773-2000, www.innatgreatneck.com)
Roslyn Claremont Hotel, Roslyn (516-625-2700, www.roslynclaremonthotel.com)

**Orient Point/Shelter Island (Latimer Reef, Little Gull Island, Long Beach
Bar, North Dumpling, Orient Point, Plum Island, Race Rock Lights)**
Other Sites of Interest:
Orient Beach State Park, Orient (631-323-2440)
Shelter Island Kayak Tours, Shelter Island (631-749-1990, www.kayaksi.com)

Lodging:
Arbor View House, East Marion (631-477-8696, www.arborviewhouse.com)
Quintessentials Bed and Breakfast Spa, East Marion (631-477-9400,
     www.quintessentialsinc.com)
The Ram's Head Inn, Shelter Island Heights (631-749-0811,
     www.shelterislandinns.com)

South Fork (Cedar Island, Montauk Point Lights)
Other Sites of Interest:
Deep Hollow Ranch, Montauk (631-668-3901, www.deephollowranch.com)
Parrish Art Museum, Southampton (631-283-2118,
     www.thehamptons.com/museum)
Sag Harbor Whaling and Historical Museum, Sag Harbor (631-725-0770,
     www.sagharborwhalingmuseum.org)
Theodore Roosevelt County Park, Montauk (631-852-7878)

Lodging:
Baron's Cove Inn, Sag Harbor (631-725-2100, www.baronscove.com)
Driftwood on the Ocean, Amagansett (631-668-5744)
East Hampton House, East Hampton (631-324-4300,
     www.easthamptonhouseresort.com)
Ocean Beach Resort at Montauk, Montauk (631-668-4000)

Southold (Horton Point Light)
Other Sites of Interest:
East End Seaport Museum, Greenport (631-477-2100, www.eastendseaport.org)
Harbes Family Farm, Mattituck (631-298-2054, www.harbesfamilyfarm.com
HMS Bounty, Greenport (631-588-7900, www.tallshipbounty.org)
Palmer Vineyards, Aquebogue (631-722-WINE, www.palmervineyards.com)
Railroad Museum of Long Island, Greenport (631-749-1990, www.bitnik.com/RMLI)

Lodging:
Coeur des Vignes L'Hotel and Restaurant Francais, Southold (631-765-2656, www.coeurdesvignes.com)
The Greenporter Hotel and Spa, Greenport (631-477-0066, www.thegreenporter.com)
Stirling House Bed and Breakfast, Greenport (631-477-0654, www.stirlinghousebandb.com)

Lighthouse Cruises and Charters

Atlantic Charters, LLC
Noank Shipyard
145 Pearl Street
Noank, CT 06340
(860) 228-1483
www.mysticsportfishing.com

DownEast Lighthouse Cruises
Pine Island Marina
Groton, CT 06340
(860) 460-1802
www.downeastlighthousecruises.com

Long Island Lighthouse Safaris
4636 Captree Island
Captree Island, NY 11702-4601
(888) 281-7071
www.lighthousesafaris.com

Mystic Whaler Cruises
P.O. Box 189
Mystic, CT 06355
(800) 697-8420
www.mysticwhaler.com

Project Oceanology
Avery Point
1804 Shennecossett Road
Groton, CT 06340
(800) 364-8472
www.oceanology.org

SeaPony **Boat Tours and Charter Cruises**
14 Eugene O'Neill Drive, Suite 202
New London, CT 06320
(860) 440-2734
www.seapony.com

Sunbeam Fleet
Captain John's Sport Fishing Center
First Street
Waterford, CT 06385
(860) 443-7259
www.sunbeamfleet.com

Sources

Carse, Robert. *Keepers of the Lights: A History of American Lighthouses*. New York: Charles Scribner's Sons, 1969.

Lewiton, Mina. *Lighthouses of America*. New York: Criterion Books, Inc., 1964.

Marcus, Jon. *Lighthouses of New England: Your Guide to the Lighthouses of Maine, New Hampshire, Vermont, Massachusetts, Rhode Island, and Connecticut*. Stillwater, Minn.: Voyageur Press, 2001.

Murray, John A., and the Lighthouse Preservation Society. *America's Lighthouses*. Lincolnwood, Ill.: Publications International, Ltd., 2002.

National Park Service, Maritime Heritage Program, Inventory of Historic Light Stations, www.cr.nps.gov/maritime/park.

Snow, Edward Rowe. *The Lighthouses of New England*, 1716–1973. New York: Dodd, Mead, 1973.

United States Coast Guard. *Light List. Volume I, Atlantic Coast from St. Croix River, Maine, to Toms River, New Jersey, First Coast Guard District*. Washington D.C.: Government Printing Office, 1999.

Works Progress Administration. *Connecticut: A Guide to Its Roads, Lore, and People*. American Guide Series. Boston: Houghton Mifflin Company, 1937.

General Lighthouse Websites:

Connecticut Lighthouses, www.unc.edu/~rowlett/lighthouse/ct.htm.
Greg's Lighthouse Page, www.thejanskys.org/lighthouse/litetop.html.
Larry's Lights, www.larryslights.com.
Lighthouse Depot, www.lhdepot.com.
Lighthouse Digest, www.lhdigest.com.
LighthouseFriends.com, www.lighthousefriends.com.
Lighthouse Getaway, www.lighthousegetaway.com.
Lighthouses: A Photographic Journey, www.ipl.org/div/light/.
Lighthouses of Long Island, New York, http://scroope.net/lighthouses/longisland.htm.
Long Island Chapter, U.S. Lighthouse Society, www.lilighthousesociety.org.
LongIslandLighthouses.com, www.longislandlighthouses.com.
National Lighthouse Museum, www.lighthousemuseum.org/harbor.htm.
National Park Service Maritime Heritage Program Inventory of Historic Light Stations, www.cr.nps.gov/maritime/ltaccess.html.
New England Lighthouses: A Virtual Guide, www.lighthouse.cc/.
New York Lighthouses, www.unc.edu/~rowlett/lighthouse/ny.htm.
United States Coast Guard Connecticut Light Stations, www.uscg.mil/hq/g-cp/history/WEBLIGHTHOUSES/LHCT.html.

Lighthouse-Specific Websites:

Avery Point Lighthouse Society, http://apls.tripod.com/.
East End Lighthouses, www.eastendlighthouses.org.
Eaton's Neck Light (Newsday.com),
    www.newsday.com/extras/lihistory/spectown/hist008j.htm.
Fire Island Lighthouse, www.fireislandlighthouse.com;
    www.newsday.com/features/custom/discover/ny-dlimosesside2.story.
Horton Point Lighthouse, www.southoldhistoricalsociety.org/lighthouse.htm.
Huntington Harbor Lighthouse, www.huntingtonlighthouse.org/.
Latimer Reef Light, www.lighthouse.cc/latimer/;
    www.rickslighthouses.com/latimer_reef.htm.
Long Beach Bar Lighthouse, www.eastendseaport.org/BugLight.htm.
Montauk Point Light, www.longislandgenealogy.com/lighthouse.html;
    www.montauktheend.com/lighthouse.html
North Dumpling Island Light, en.wikipedia.org/wiki/North_Dumpling_Island.
Sheffield Island Lighthouse, www.seaport.org.
    www.greenport.com/lighthouses/welcome.htm#anchor2100248 (East End
    lighthouses).

Other Websites:

Fire Island National Seashore, www.nps.gov/fiis/.
GhostlyPlaces.com, www.e-clipse.com/gp/newyork.htm.
http://dep.state.ct.us/olisp/licplate/licbenefits.htm.
http://town.huntington.ny.us/.
LongIsland.com, www.longisland.com.
Long Island Genealogy, www.longislandgenealogy.com/barnabas/barna001.htm.
Newsday.com, www.newsday.com/extras/lihistory/spectown/hist0055.htm.
Squire Frederick Chase and the Place Called Prospect, www.shelter-island.org/chase/
    lighthouse.html
Suffolk Life Newspapers, "Ghost Hunters Reveal Haunted L.I. Locales,"
    www.zwire.com/site/news.cfm?newsid=5876971&BRD=1776&PAG=461&dept_
    id=6365&rfi=8
Wired Magazine, Issue 8.09, www.wired.com/wired/archive/8.09/kamen_pr.html.
www.fireisland.com.

All directions to Connecticut lighthouses are taken from www.lhdepot.com and are used with permission from the author. Special thanks to the American Lighthouse Foundation's Tim Harrison and Jeremy D'Entremont for their permission to use this and other information from the site.

About the Photographer

Paul Rezendes is the photographer of Tide-mark's "Lighthouse Companion Series," including *The Lighthouse Companion for Long Island Sound*; *The Lighthouse Companion for Massachusetts, Rhode Island, and New Hampshire*; and *The Lighthouse Companion for Maine*. He is also the photographer of *Martha's Vineyard Seasons*, also published by Tide-mark.

Rezendes's other books include the highly acclaimed guide *Tracking & the Art of Seeing: How to Read Animal Tracks and Sign; Wetlands: The Web of Life*, coauthored with his wife, Paulette M. Roy; and *The Wild Within: Adventures in Nature and Animal Teachings*. His photographs have appeared in hundreds of calendars, magazines, books, and catalogs; on posters and cards; and in brochures and promotional materials for corporate and commercial accounts in the United States and abroad. He has worked on assignment for several regional and national magazines, and operates his own stock photography business. A native New Englander, Paul grew up in Westport, Massachusetts, and lives with his wife in a remote forest on the banks of the Millers River in Athol, Massachusetts.

For more information, please contact:

Paul Rezendes Photography
3833 Bearsden Road
Royalston, MA 01368-9400
USA

Tel: (978) 249-8810
e-mail: photos@paulrezendes.com
Website: www.paulrezendes.com